Contents

Listen

Praying in a
Noisy World

Rueben P. Job

Abingdon Press
Nashville

LISTEN
Praying in a Noisy World

By Rueben P. Job

Library of Congress Cataloging-in-Publication applied for.

ISBN 9781426780745

14 15 16 17 18 19 20 21 22 23—10 9 8 7 6 5 4 3 2
Manufactured in the United States of America

Introduction

It was a mystical moment for Peter, James, and John as they saw Jesus transformed before their eyes and then saw him speaking to Moses and Elijah. They were so moved by their experience that they wanted to build shrines to Jesus, Moses, and Elijah. But before they could build anything, they were interrupted by a voice that said, "This is my Son, whom I dearly love. Listen to him!" (Mark 9:7).

We, like the disciples before us, sometimes forget that our relationship with God begins and ends in listening. In our noisy and busy world, it is not surprising that we forget this elementary truth. The remedy is not to deny this truth or to scold ourselves or to take on unnecessary loads of guilt. Rather, the remedy lies in learning again the habit of listening to God in all things and at all times. Each day of our lives can become an exquisite communication system of listening to, learning from, and responding to God in every moment of every day in which we are given the gift of life.

Everyone who reads these words has been created by God not only to listen for God but also to hear and understand God's communication with us. Prayer and discernment, which is the ability to sense or hear God's guidance and communication, are not gifts for special people only. They are gifts for all people.

Prayer is the pathway for a vital, growing, and fulfilling relationship with God. When our relationship with God is healthy, prayer and discernment are natural consequences of our daily companionship with God's Holy Spirit. We must rely first on the ever-present Spirit of God, not on particular methods or models of prayer and discernment, for guidance, direction, and companionship. Through the Spirit, we have within us—just as we are—the capacity to develop an intimate, lasting, and fulfilling relationship with the God revealed most clearly in the life of Jesus Christ. Likewise, we have been given the capacity to listen for and faithfully respond to God's guidance and direction for every decision we will ever face.

As those who seek to follow Jesus, we want to deepen our relationship with God and learn to know and do God's will. We know this is the path of faithful and fruitful living. Yet often we think that knowing and doing God's will is over our heads, or we find it so very hard to do because we think it requires gifts, time, and capacity that we simply do not have.

Listen seeks to assist you in moving from being one who lives with these self-imposed limitations to being one who knows not

6

only how to pray but also how to listen, understand, and follow God's guidance and direction. *Listen* has been created to assist individuals, small groups, and congregations in the quest to discover our full inheritance as children of God and, after this discovery, to live as joyful and faithful children of God.

Ideal for use during Lent or any time of year, this book is designed to be used every day for a period of forty days so that we may learn to listen anew and to acquire the habits that lead to a deep and vital relationship with God, resulting in life-giving patterns of prayer and discernment. As we learn to listen, we learn to pray; and as we learn to pray in response to our listening, we will learn to discern what the living God is saying and where God desires to lead us.

This process of listening, praying, and discerning begins with recognizing who we are and to whom we belong. The apostle Paul put it this way:

> *I pray that the God of our Lord Jesus Christ, the Father of glory, will give you a spirit of wisdom and revelation that makes God known to you. I pray that the eyes of your heart will have enough light to see what is the hope of God's call, what is the richness of God's glorious inheritance among believers, and what is the overwhelming greatness of God's power that is working among us believers. This power is conferred by the energy of God's powerful strength.*

Ephesians 1:17-19

In her book *In Ordinary Time*, Roberta Bondi describes the core of who we are with these words:

> Before anything else, above all else, beyond everything else, God loves us. God loves us extravagantly, ridiculously, without limit or condition. God is in love with us; God is besotted with us. God yearns for us. God does not love us "in spite of who we are" or "for whom God knows we can become." According to the wonderful fourth- and fifth-century teachers I have learned from and also teach myself, God loves us hopelessly as mothers love their babies . . . even against what we ourselves sometimes find plausible, God likes us.

Bondi goes on to affirm that we are made in the image of God and "made for the purpose of knowing and loving God and one another and of being loved in turn, not literally in the same way God knows and loves, but in a way appropriate to human beings."

Learning to listen and pray in a noisy world begins with knowing that we were created by God for the purpose of knowing and loving God and others. The purpose of our listening, then, is both personal and communal, encompassing the well-being of our neighbor.

Vaclav Havel said, "the salvation of this human world lies nowhere else than in the human heart." As we practice the disciplines of prayer and discernment, we seek not only personal salvation but also the salvation of the world that God created and loves. Havel's words are a reminder that we, too, have a part in the salvation of the world; our relationship with God is not only for our benefit but also for the benefit of the world. Therefore, this resource is not only for the benefit of the individuals, congregations, and small groups that will use it; my prayer is that it also will lead to transformational moments that result in new efforts to expose God's transforming presence, purpose, and power to the world in which we live.

Rueben P. Job

How to Use This Book

Jesus often sought silence and solitude to pray and seek his beloved Abba's direction. No matter where we are in our busy and noisy world, we can do the same, but it will take practice, patience, and perseverance. They say that it takes forty days to develop a habit. This is your invitation to walk with me through the next forty days as we develop our ability to position ourselves to be more fully available to God, while seeking to live as faithful disciples of Jesus Christ. Whether you are joining me on your own or as a member of a small group or congregation using *Listen* as a study or devotional guide during Lent or another time of year, together we will learn and practice the habits that will deepen our relationship with God and enhance our ability to hear and respond to God's guidance.

The number forty has special significance in the Bible. Three unforgettable examples are the forty years the Israelites spent wandering in the wilderness trying to learn how to live by the promises of God (Deuteronomy 2:7), the forty days when Jesus was tempted in the wilderness following his baptism and God's declaration that he was indeed God's Son (Mark 1:10-11), and the forty days between the resurrection and the ascension of Jesus that was a time of intense learning for the disciples (Acts 1:3).

Like each of those forty-day experiences, this forty-day journey we are undertaking will not be without some risk. It may be a time of separating the wheat from the chaff as we determine again where our love for God and our love for neighbor rank in our lives. It surely will be a time of practicing the habits of faithfulness to God's call, which requires surrender and perseverance. It even may be a time of decision as we consider our commitment to walking with Jesus and the cost of following where he leads. However, I believe that the enormous potential in this forty-day journey surpasses any risk. If we are open, diligent, and faithful, we will learn to live a life of prayer and discernment that will far exceed all that we have yet discovered or experienced.

This quest of seeking God's presence and direction may seem overwhelming until we remember that Jesus told us we would have all the help we need in discovering what we must know in order to live fully as his disciples. He said, "The Companion, the Holy Spirit, whom the Father will send in my name, will teach you everything and will remind you of everything I told you" (John 14:26). We are not left on our own to learn how to pray or how to discern God's will; our Companion, the Holy Spirit, is our teacher and guide as we learn how to live more faithfully and fully in relationship with God. It is

God who chooses to make our way known to us, and it is God who does the revealing, leading, and instructing.

Our greatest challenge will be to learn to listen to the many ways in which God is speaking to us all the time—through Scripture, creation, history, current events, the stories of others and of our own lives, and the moments of our daily existence—and then to trust that the Holy Spirit desires to guide us as we learn how to pray and discern God's purpose and will for us in every situation. In other words, we will have the Master Teacher as our tutor for the rest of our lives—a teacher with all knowledge and compassion and the desire to see us live life fully, joyfully, productively, and faithfully. What a wonderful promise as we begin our journey of discovery!

Every day of our journey we will invite our Companion to help us learn from each daily experience, each daily reading, and each life story, including our own. May we accept each source of revelation as a special gift that the Master Teacher desires to use to show us the way forward, to make us whole, and to fill us with the joy, peace, and creativity that lead to a fulfilling life.

The Weekly Sections

This book will serve as our guide on our forty-day journey. It is divided into six weekly plans, each including the following sections:

Prayer Practice	A featured prayer technique or habit for the week. Read through the prayer practice at the beginning of the week. The practice will be incorporated in some part of the Daily Prayer Pattern and highlighted in the weekly group session.
Daily Prayer Pattern	A pattern or liturgy for a daily time of prayer and reflection.
Daily Scriptures	Scripture readings for each day of the week.
Weekly Reading	A story or reflection to read on the first day of the week and to ponder throughout the week.

Interspersed throughout these sections, you will find thought-provoking quotations to supplement and enrich your reading. Use them during the Reading segment of the prayer pattern as well as at other times to prompt your reflection and response.

The Daily Prayer Pattern

The prayer pattern or liturgy that you will follow each day is simple and straightforward in its design. It is intended to help bring you into God's presence more fully each time it becomes your path of prayer for the day. When you are deeply aware that you are in God's presence, you will be guided in your life of prayer and discernment.

The following paragraphs will introduce you to the various segments of the prayer pattern we are using for this forty-day immersion in God's presence. Feel free to make adjustments and adapt this pattern as you see fit to meet your own personal needs and schedule. Each of us is a unique creation of God, and our methods of prayer will not be identical. The important thing is to establish a daily pattern of prayer that is comfortable and fruitful for your personal walk with God. Whatever pattern you use will be the practice field for listening, hearing, and responding to the voice of God made known in Jesus Christ.

Prayer of Presence

How do we receive and treat a most honored guest? With care, respect, and reverence. That is the way we are to approach our time of prayer and reflection. We are to make careful preparation for our honored guest and give our full and undivided attention to the presence of the One who has come among us for this special time together.

Preparing to enter into God's presence is the first movement in any effort to learn to listen for and seek God's guidance and direction. The Psalms carry this message again and again, and we pray with them:

> *O God, you are my God, I seek you,*
> *my soul thirsts for you;*
> *my flesh faints for you,*
> *as in a dry and weary land where there is no water.*
> Psalm 63:1 NRSV

In his book *Man Is Not Alone*, Jewish mystic Abraham J. Heschel said, "God is of no importance unless he is of supreme importance." So we begin our time of prayer and discernment by consciously inviting God's presence and immersing ourselves in that presence before we do anything else. At first this may seem to be an awkward or insignificant movement in our life of prayer. My witness is similar to many others who, after years of practice, acknowledge that inviting God's presence has become a wonderful and essential habit that often opens new windows to God's presence that, once discovered, we are very reluctant to close.

As you prepare for your time of prayer, seek a quiet place. Use the words provided to invite God's presence. Repeat this opening prayer each day, or modify the prayer with your own words as you move through the week. As you pray, open your heart and mind to recognize and welcome God's presence and to hear and respond to God's call.

Silence

In our noisy world, we spend very little time in silence and solitude. After acknowledging and inviting God's presence, take a moment to sit in silence. This is a time to quiet the noise around you and heed the call to "be still, and know that I am God!" (Psalm 46:10 NRSV). Shift your focus from exterior concerns to the interior life. Empty your mind of other voices so that you may hear the divine voice.

A few words of instruction are provided to guide you in this time. As you focus your thoughts on God's presence, become aware of the gift from God that you are about to unwrap, open, and enjoy. Sit in silence for a few moments, lengthening the time each day if you are able. With practice and persistence, you will find that it will become easier to be silent and still for longer periods of time. You will begin to look forward to this time of quieting your soul before God.

Scripture

Scripture has always been at the heart of God's revelation and central to the life of the Christian and the church. It is where we go to hear God's personal message to us and where, through the stories of God's mighty acts and the parables of Jesus, we see and hear truth about God's kingdom and will and see God's very self revealed as in no other place.

A Scripture reading is suggested for each day. These texts have been selected to support and enhance the theme for the week. Whether you begin on Monday or another day of the week, use this list to guide your reading of God's Word throughout the week. Feel free to supplement with additional Scriptures that speak to a similar theme.

For ease of use, each week you will find the printed Scripture texts from the Common English Bible in the Daily Scriptures section. Simply turn to that section to read the Scripture for the day and then continue the Daily Prayer Pattern.

Reading

Each week a story or reflection is provided to prompt further contemplation of the week's theme. Each story comes from ordinary people and real life experiences. Approach the story with the same openness and respect that you offer to any special guest you invite into your presence. Pay attention to the details of the story and the main truth it contains. Look for ways in which the story on the page relates to the story of your life.

It is suggested that you read the story on the first day of your week and ponder it throughout the week. You will find the story in the Weekly Reading section. After reading the story, move on to the next segment of the Daily Prayer Pattern.

Each day of the week when you come to this part of the prayer pattern, recall the story and consider any new insights or applications. You also may supplement this part of your prayer exercise each day with additional readings, drawing upon the quotations that are sprinkled throughout the week. If it is helpful to you, you may want to write the date beside each quotation as you read it.

Dialogue and Discovery

Now that you have read Scripture and story, it is time to consider what questions, insights, and revelations these readings have raised or revealed. This is a time to enter into dialogue with the Spirit of God, inviting God to speak as you reflect on the questions provided. This exercise goes hand in hand with the Reflection and Response sections that follow.

Reflection

As you reflect on the Dialogue and Discovery questions, note any insights here in the Reflection section. This space is your own to record your thoughts as you dialogue with God. If you need additional space, turn to the journaling pages provided at the end of the book.

Response

Now it is time to move from reflecting to responding. In your response time, you are invited to write what action the various sources of revelation are prompting you to take. Space is provided for recording your urgings, cautions, encouragements, and discouragements, as well as how you have decided to respond to the "signs and signals" you have heard or observed. If you need additional space, turn to the journaling pages provided at the end of the book.

Prayers of Petition

During this time, give thanks for God's sustaining and revealing grace as you follow the prayer prompts that have been provided, commending to God's care the needs of the world and its leaders and people, including your own needs. Conclude this time of petition with the perfect prayer that Jesus taught his disciples to pray, the Lord's Prayer (see page 26).

Blessing

A blessing is provided to end your daily practice of prayer. As you read the blessing (aloud if possible), remember that you receive and take God's blessing with you into the day or time ahead.

Jesus replied, "The most important one is Israel, listen! Our God is the one Lord, and you must love the Lord your God with all your heart, with all your being, with all your mind, and with all your strength. The second is this, You will love your neighbor as yourself. No other commandment is greater than these."

Mark 12:29-31

Prayer Practice

Sitting in Silence

As we seek to listen and pray in a noisy world, it is appropriate and necessary to learn to sit in silence. Sitting in silence helps to prepare our hearts and minds for communion with God, allowing us to become more aware of God's presence with us. This week you are encouraged to make the practice of sitting in silence a focal part of your prayer time.

Begin by sitting quietly and comfortably. Allow the exterior voices to be silenced as you focus on the interior voice of God, who is seeking your attention. Some use a physical item such as a cross or icon to assist them in reaching this place of silence where the gentle voice of God's Spirit may be heard, understood, and obeyed. If your mind wanders or you are distracted, gently return your focus to God's interior voice.

With persistence and practice, sitting in silence will become more and more comfortable and natural, and you will look forward to this time of quieting your soul before God.

God speaks to us in the everyday language and experiences of life. When we listen, we will not only learn to trust God's guidance in discernment but will learn to trust God and God's love in all things and at all times. What a wonderful gift to those who are attentive!

Rueben P. Job

THIS IS MY SON, LISTEN TO HIM

Daily Prayer Pattern

Prayer of Presence

> *Holy God*
> > *of unconditional love*
> > *and unlimited presence,*
> > *I come to make myself fully available*
> > *to you, your will, and your way.*
> *Speak to me gently and clearly,*
> > *for I am yours*
> > *and desire to hear, understand,*
> > *and be obedient*
> > *to your slightest whisper.*
> *Speak, for I am listening.*

Silence

Now is the time to incorporate the week's focal prayer practice of sitting in silence. Wait in silence as you invite the Spirit's guidance to form your prayers and shape your life. Quiet your soul before God for several minutes, extending the time a little more each day if possible.

Scripture

Monday	Mark 1:9-13
Tuesday	Matthew 17:1-6
Wednesday	Mark 9:1-8
Thursday	Isaiah 1:16-18
Friday	Luke 9:28-35
Saturday	John 8:31-38
Sunday	2 Peter 1:16-21

Turn to the Daily Scriptures section to read the day's text from the Common English Bible.

Reading

On the first day of your week, read the story found in the Weekly Reading section. Pay attention to the details of the story and the main truth it contains. Look for ways in which the story on the page relates to the story of your life.

On each day following, recall the story and consider any new insights or applications. You also may choose to read and reflect on the quotations interspersed throughout Week 1.

Dialogue and Discovery

What is the Scripture passage saying to me today?
Can I accept and apply this message to myself? To my world?
How will this message change my life?
What is the reading revealing to me today?

What messages does the reading call forth from my own story?
What direction, guidance, or wisdom am I hearing and sensing?
What actions are being suggested as my response?

Reflection
Insights and Thoughts:

Response
Today I will ...

Prayers of Petition
For the world, its leaders, and its people
For those whose lives touch mine today
For myself and those placed in my care
The prayer Jesus taught us

Blessing
   God of love and compassion, grant me grace to walk in companionship with you this day so that I may hear and respond to your call and walk in faithfulness and peace this day and always.

The Lord's Prayer

The Prayer That Jesus Taught Us

Our Father, which art in heaven,
Hallowed be thy Name.
Thy Kingdom come.
Thy will be done in earth,
As it is in heaven.

Give us this day our daily bread.
And forgive us our trespasses,
As we forgive them that trespass against us.
And lead us not into temptation,
But deliver us from evil.
For thine is the kingdom,
The power, and the glory,
For ever and ever.
Amen.

Daily Scriptures

Monday   *Mark 1:9-13*

About that time, Jesus came from Nazareth of Galilee, and John baptized him in the Jordan River. While he was coming up out of the water, Jesus saw heaven splitting open and the Spirit, like a dove, coming down on him. And there was a voice from heaven: "You are my Son, whom I dearly love; in you I find happiness."

At once the Spirit forced Jesus out into the wilderness. He was in the wilderness for forty days, tempted by Satan. He was among the wild animals, and the angels took care of him.

Tuesday   *Matthew 17:1-6*

Six days later Jesus took Peter, James, and John his brother, and brought them to the top of a very high mountain. He was transformed in front of them. His face shone like the sun, and his clothes became as white as light.

Moses and Elijah appeared to them, talking with Jesus. Peter reacted to all of this by saying to Jesus, "Lord, it's good that we're here. If you want, I'll make three shrines: one for you, one for Moses, and one for Elijah."

While he was still speaking, look, a bright cloud over-shadowed them. A voice from the cloud said, "This is my Son whom I dearly love. I am very pleased with him. Listen to him!" Hearing this, the disciples fell on their faces, filled with awe.

Christians at their best are good listeners, and the Christian church, when most faithful, is a listening community. To live with God in this world that God loves requires some intense and intentional listing. So many competing voices are calling for our attention that without concentrated effort and determination we may easily miss what God is saying to us. We may even miss the way and will into which God is trying to lead us.

Rueben P. Job, *A Guide to Spiritual Discernment*

❦

Wednesday   *Mark 9:1-8*

Jesus continued, "I assure you that some standing here won't die before they see God's kingdom arrive in power."

Six days later Jesus took Peter, James, and John, and brought them to the top of a very high mountain where they were alone. He was transformed in front of them, and his clothes were amazingly bright, brighter than if they had been bleached white. Elijah and Moses appeared and were talking with Jesus. Peter reacted to all of this by saying to Jesus, "Rabbi, it's good that we're here. Let's make three shrines— one for you, one for Moses, and one for Elijah." He said this because he didn't know how to respond, for the three of them were terrified.

Then a cloud overshadowed them, and a voice spoke from the cloud, "This is my Son, whom I dearly love. Listen to him!" Suddenly, looking around, they no longer saw anyone with them except Jesus.

Thursday   *Isaiah 1:16-18*

Wash! Be clean!
Remove your ugly deeds from my sight.
Put an end to such evil;
learn to do good.
Seek justice:
help the oppressed;
defend the orphan;
plead for the widow.

Come now, and let's settle this,
says the LORD.

Though your sins are like scarlet,
    they will be white as snow.
If they are red as crimson,
    they will become like wool.

❧

Friday   *Luke 9:28-35*

About eight days after Jesus said these things, he took Peter, John, and James, and went up on a mountain to pray. As he was praying, the appearance of his face changed and his clothes flashed white like lightning. Two men, Moses and Elijah, were talking with him. They were clothed with heavenly splendor and spoke about Jesus' departure, which he would achieve in Jerusalem. Peter and those with him were almost overcome by sleep, but they managed to stay awake and saw his glory as well as the two men with him.

As the two men were about to leave Jesus, Peter said to him, "Master, it's good that we're here. We should construct three shrines: one for you, one for Moses, and one for Elijah"—but he didn't know what he was saying. Peter was still speaking when a cloud overshadowed them. As they entered the cloud, they were overcome with awe.

Then a voice from the cloud said, "This is my Son, my chosen one. Listen to him!"

Theological reflection is reflecting on the painful and joyful realities of every day with the mind of Jesus and thereby raising human consciousness to the knowledge of God's gentle guidance. This is a hard discipline, since God's presence is often a hidden presence, a presence that needs to be discovered. The loud, boisterous noises of the world make us deaf to the soft, gentle, and loving voice of God.

Henri Nouwen, *In the Name of Jesus*

Saturday   *John 8:31-38*

Jesus said to the Jews who believed in him, "You are truly my disciples if you remain faithful to my teaching. Then you will know the truth, and the truth will set you free."

They responded, "We are Abraham's children; we've never been anyone's slaves. How can you say that we will be set free?"

Jesus answered, "I assure you that everyone who sins is a slave to sin. A slave isn't a permanent member of the household, but a son is. Therefore, if the Son makes you free, you really will be free. I know that you are Abraham's children, yet you want to kill me because you don't welcome my teaching. I'm telling you what I've seen when I am with the Father, but you are doing what you've heard from your father."

꽃

Sunday   *2 Peter 1:16-21*

We didn't repeat crafty myths when we told you about the powerful coming of our Lord Jesus Christ. Quite the contrary, we witnessed his majesty with our own eyes. He received honor and glory from God the Father when a voice came to him from the magnificent glory, saying, "This is my dearly loved Son, with whom I am well-pleased." We ourselves heard this voice from heaven while we were with him on the holy mountain. In addition, we have a most reliable prophetic word, and you would do well to pay attention to it, just as you would to a lamp shining in a dark place, until the day dawns and the morning star rises in your hearts. Most important, you must know that no prophecy of scripture represents the prophet's own understanding of things, because no prophecy ever came by human will. Instead, men and women led by the Holy Spirit spoke from God.

Weekly Reading

As a child I loved to spend warm summer days playing near where a freshwater spring brought cool water to a deep and long ravine surrounded by gently rising tall hills. While our dog, my constant companion, was hunting for frogs, I was exploring red-winged blackbird nests and tiny minnows that washed in with the spring snow melt, enjoying the cool water on my bare feet.

Of course, I had no watch, and now and then I would be lost in the mystery of that inviting space and miss my mother's call to the evening meal. If I was paying attention, I could usually hear her call even though our house was about a quarter of a mile away. But when I was not paying attention or listening for her voice, especially if the wind was blowing, there were times when I missed her call.

A follow-up to her call was to send one of my older brothers to bring me home. Their disappointment and displeasure at having to walk partway to get a wayward younger brother for the evening meal was often clearly expressed as we walked to the house, and I soon learned the high price of not listening and paying attention to a very important voice. It is easy to get focused on any number of things and miss out on hearing the most important voice we will ever hear.

Today it is very hard to hear the gentle voice of God in the loud and noisy culture in which we live. Sometimes we all need help, not only to listen but also to hear. The good news is that there is help available. The simple habit of following the rhythm of prayer that we are using as we live out these forty days of discovery can open our lives to the wonderful and surprising conversation that God seeks to have with each of us.

The truth is that sometimes we need help to hear.

Once when I was responsible for my grandchild's bedtime and naptime, I discovered a practice that almost guaranteed a successful time of rest. When I held him with his head near my heart, he always became quiet and relaxed. We figured out that the earliest memories he had were of his mother's heartbeat. When everything else seemed frightening, the rhythm of my heartbeat gave him confidence, comfort, and peaceful rest.

Today, how do we intend to hear the heartbeat of God? What will we do to make it possible for us to hear God's comforting, peace-giving, and guiding voice?

Rueben P. Job

Prayer Practice

Releasing Our Fears, Needs, and Hopes

Bringing our fears, needs, and hopes to God in prayer helps us to establish intimacy with God and hear God's voice. Yet releasing our uncertainties to God's care often does not come easily. As we grow to trust God's love and presence, we find this practice to be easier.

As a child, I was cradled in my father's lap during a long and serious illness. It was then that I learned that love overcomes fear and offers hope, even in difficult and frightening times. Nearly eighty years later, I know with confidence that the reality of God's love and promise to never forsake us provides these same gifts.

This week you are encouraged to practice releasing your fears, needs, and hopes into God's care. As you do, invite the Spirit to reassure you of God's love and presence. If anxious thoughts return, take them to God as soon as you are conscious of them and give thanks for God's faithful presence, love, and care. Do this as often as necessary, and you will find that your fears subside as your confidence in God's faithfulness grows.

Whenever I feel my foot slipping, your faithful love steadies me, Lord.
When my anxieties multiply, your comforting calms me down.

Psalm 94:18-19

To live without prayer is to live without God, to live without a soul.

Abraham J. Heschel, *Between God and Man*

PRAY LIKE THIS

Daily Prayer Pattern

Prayer of Presence

Each day this week, begin your time of prayer with the practice of releasing your fears, needs, and hopes to God. Use this prayer to acknowledge God's presence and love, and then follow the prompt to surrender your concerns to God.

Loving God,
Who understands before I form my prayer,
Who hears when I call and translates my humble words
*   into beautiful hymns of gratitude and praise*
And responds to my uncertain cry for help
*   with assurance, peace, and palpable presence,*

Here I am as fully in your presence
*   as I am able to be,*
Offering my fears, my needs, my hopes,
*   my love, and my life,*
For I am yours and belong to no other.

At this time, name your fears, needs, and hopes, entrusting them to God's care. As you give your concerns to God, give thanks for God's constant and unfailing love and presence.

Visualize God's loving arms enfolding you.

Silence

Wait in silence as you invite the Spirit's guidance to form your prayers and shape your life. Allow the exterior noises and voices to be silenced as you focus on the interior voice of God.

Scripture

Monday	Luke 11:1-10
Tuesday	Job 22: 21-30
Wednesday	Mark 6:37-44
Thursday	Matthew 6:7-15
Friday	Psalm 46:1-7
Saturday	Mark 14:32-38
Sunday	John 17:20-24

Turn to the Daily Scriptures section to read the day's text from the Common English Bible.

Reading

On the first day of your week, read the story found in the Weekly Reading section. Pay attention to the details of the story and the main truth it contains. Look for ways in which the story on the page relates to the story of your life.

On each day following, recall the story and consider any

new insights or applications. You also may choose to read and reflect on the quotations interspersed throughout Week 2.

Dialogue and Discovery
What is the Scripture passage saying to me today?
Can I accept and apply this message to myself? To my world?
How will this message change my life?
What is the reading revealing to me today?
What messages does the reading call forth from my own story?
What direction, guidance, or wisdom am I hearing and sensing?
What actions are being suggested as my response?

Reflection
Insights and thoughts:

Response
Today I will ...

Prayers of Petition
For the world, its leaders, and its people
For those whose lives touch mine today
For myself and those placed in my care
The prayer Jesus taught us

Blessing
 I will accept and cherish my relationship as a beloved and loving child of God as I live a life of prayer in God's presence today.

Jesus teaches us that prayer is fundamentally a loving listening to God as he continually communicates his love to us at each movement. We pray when we are attentive to the presence of God.

When we lift our hearts and minds to God's communicating presence, God does not begin and then cease to enter into this loving self-giving. His Son, Jesus, realized in his prayer that his Father surrounded him at every moment of his earthly existence with his Spirit. He opened himself to receive that "invasion" of his Father's goodness by yielding actively to whatever the Father was asking of him in each moment. Thus, Jesus prayed always in whatever he was engaged in doing.

Prayer, for Jesus, was not an activity in which he engaged before he did something else. It was a permanent, ever-increasing state of being turned inwardly toward the Father at every moment in loving trust and self-surrender. Prayer became synonymous with loving surrender based on childlike trust.

George A. Maloney, *In Jesus We Trust*

Listen, my people, to my teaching;
  tilt your ears toward the words of my mouth.
  Psalm 78:1

Daily Scriptures

Jesus was praying in a certain place. When he finished, one of his disciples said, "Lord, teach us to pray, just as John taught his disciples."

Jesus told them, "When you pray, say:

'Father, uphold the holiness of your name.
Bring in your kingdom.
Give us the bread we need for today.
Forgive us our sins,
    for we also forgive everyone who has wronged us.
And don't lead us into temptation.' "

He also said to them, "Imagine that one of you has a friend and you go to that friend in the middle of the night. Imagine saying, 'Friend, loan me three loaves of bread because a friend of mine on a journey has arrived and I have nothing to set before him.' Imagine further that he answers from within the house, 'Don't bother me. The door is already locked, and my children and I are in bed. I can't get up to give you anything.' I assure you, even if he wouldn't get up and help because of his friendship, he will get up and give his friend whatever he needs because of his friend's brashness. And I tell you: Ask and you will receive. Seek and you will find. Knock and the door will be opened to you. Everyone who asks, receives. Whoever seeks, finds. To everyone who knocks, the door is opened."

Perhaps the most startling thought that can inhabit the human imagination is that a man or a woman, earthbound and stuttering, can speak meaningfully to God.

Ben Campbell Johnson, *GodSpeech*

❦

Tuesday   *Job 22:21-30*

Get along well with God and be at peace;
       from this something good
              will come to you.
Receive instruction from his mouth;
       put his words in your mind.
If you return to the Almighty,
       you will be restored;
       if you keep wrongdoing
              out of your tent.
Lay your prized possession in the dust,

your gold from Ophir on a rock
    in a desert streambed.
The Almighty will be your
    prized possession,
    silver piled up for you.
Then you will take pleasure
    in the Almighty;
    lift up your face to God.
You will pray to him, and he will hear you;
    you will fulfill your solemn promises.
If you decree something, it will stand;
    light will shine on your ways.
When they're humbled, you will say:
    "Cheer up;
    God will rescue the lowly.
    He will deliver the guilty;
    they will be saved by your pure hands."

I'd like to say something a bit different about prayer, and therefore about religion. Prayer is not primarily saying words or thinking thoughts. It is rather a stance. It's a way of living in the Presence. It is, further, a way of living in awareness of the Presence, even enjoying the Presence. The full contemplative is not just aware of the Presence, but trusts, allows and delights in it.

Richard Rohr, *Everything Belongs*

Wednesday   *Mark 6:37-44*

He replied, "You give them something to eat."

But they said to him, "Should we go off and buy bread worth almost eight months' pay and give it to them to eat?"

He said to them, "How much bread do you have? Take a look."

After checking, they said, "Five loaves of bread and two fish."

He directed the disciples to seat all the people in groups as though they were having a banquet on the green grass. They sat down in groups of hundreds and fifties. He took the five loaves and the two fish, looked up to heaven, blessed them, broke the loaves into pieces, and gave them to his disciples to set before the people. He also divided the two fish among them all. Everyone ate until they were full. They filled twelve baskets with the leftover pieces of bread and fish. About five thousand had eaten.

O begin! Fix some part of every day for private exercises. . . . Do justice to your own soul; give it time and means to grow. Do not starve yourself any longer.

John Wesley, "Letter to Mr. John Trembath"

Thursday   *Matthew 6:7-15*

"When you pray, don't pour out a flood of empty words, as the Gentiles do. They think that by saying many words they'll be heard. Don't be like them, because your Father knows what you need before you ask. Pray like this:

> Our Father who is in heaven,
>> uphold the holiness of your name.
> Bring in your kingdom
>> so that your will is done on earth
>> as it's done in heaven.
> Give us the bread we need for today.
> Forgive us for the ways we have wronged you,
>> just as we also forgive those who have wronged us.
> And don't lead us into temptation,
>> but rescue us from the evil one.

"If you forgive others their sins, your heavenly Father will also forgive you. But if you don't forgive others, neither will your Father forgive your sins."

🦋

Friday   *Psalm 46:1-7*

God is our refuge and strength,
    a help always near
           in times of great trouble.
That's why we won't be afraid
    when the world falls apart,
    when the mountains crumble into the
           center of the sea,
    when its waters roar and rage,
    when the mountains shake
           because of its surging waves.   Selah

There is a river whose streams
    gladden God's city,
    the holiest dwelling of the Most High.
God is in that city. It will never crumble.
    God will help it when morning dawns.
Nations roar; kingdoms crumble.
    God utters his voice; the earth melts.
The LORD of heavenly forces is with us!
    The God of Jacob is our place of safety.   Selah

Saturday   *Mark 14:32-38*

Jesus and his disciples came to a place called Gethsemane. Jesus said to them, "Sit here while I pray." He took Peter, James, and John along with him. He began to feel despair and was anxious. He said to them, "I'm very sad. It's as if I'm dying. Stay here and keep alert." Then he went a short distance farther and fell to the ground. He prayed that, if possible, he might be spared the time of suffering. He said, "Abba, Father, for you all things are possible. Take this cup of suffering away from me. However—not what I want but what you want."

He came and found them sleeping. He said to Peter, "Simon, are you asleep? Couldn't you stay alert for one hour? Stay alert and pray so that you won't give in to temptation. The spirit is eager, but the flesh is weak."

Sunday   *John 17:20-24*

"I'm not praying only for them but also for those who believe in me because of their word. I pray they will be one, Father, just as you are in me and I am in you. I pray that they also will be in us, so that the world will believe that you sent me. I've given them the glory that you gave me so that they can be one just as we are one. I'm in them and you are in me so that they will be made perfectly one. Then the world will know that you sent me and that you have loved them just as you loved me.

"Father, I want those you gave me to be with me where I am. Then they can see my glory, which you gave me because you loved me before the creation of the world."

Weekly Reading

Having celebrated my eighty-fifth birthday, I have practiced a life of prayer for a long time. However, the truth is that I am still learning how to pray. Of course, it could be no other way. Prayer grows out of and is built upon God's relationship with us and our relationship with God. And since God is infinite, why would we think that we could know everything about prayer? What we can become is faithful children of God who are led into an ever-deepening relationship with God and deeper levels of prayer.

Sometimes we are frightened away from our own prayer practices or even from beginning a life of prayer by others who talk about prayer in lofty terms that we do not understand. There are indeed many ways of prayer and many aids to prayer, but in reality prayer at its foundation is quite simple and open and available to everyone.

In response to the request of the disciples, Jesus taught them a simple and profound prayer. We call this prayer the Lord's Prayer. It captured the essence of the relationship Jesus had with his beloved Abba, and it continues to be the central model prayer of followers of Jesus today.

Prayer is not meant to be complicated, complex, and left to professionals. Prayer is for all of us. It is simply offering the fears, needs, hopes, longings, and questions of our minds and hearts to God as honestly, earnestly, and accurately as we can. Our prayers also express the essence of who we are and what our relationship is with God. Yet it is not our initiative that begins our prayer. Rather, it is God's seeking love and invitation that awaken within us the desire, courage, and need to pray.

It is encouraging to remember that prayer is not all up to us. God is always pursuing us, always trying to get our attention, always seeking relationship with us. Best of all, as Paul declares, the Holy Spirit assists us every step of the way: "We don't know what we should pray, but the Spirit himself pleads our case" (Romans 8:26).

If you have the desire to pray, you already have everything it takes to live a life of prayer. Permit the Spirit to guide you as you pray and as you journey deeper into a life of prayer.

Today the heart of God is an open wound of love. He aches over our distance and preoccupation. He mourns that we do not draw near to him. He grieves that we have forgotten him. He weeps over our obsession with muchness and manyness. He longs for our presence.

And he is inviting you and me to come home to where we belong, to come home to that for which we were created. His arms are stretched out and wide to receive us. His heart is enlarged to take us in.

For too long we have been in the far country; a country of noise and hurry and crowds, a country of climb and push and shove, a country of frustration and fear and intimidation. And he welcomes us home: home to serenity and peace and joy, home to friendship and fellowship and openness, home to intimacy and acceptance and affirmation.

Richard Foster, *Prayer: Finding the Heart's True Home*

Prayer Practice

Intentional Listening

Learning to live in communion with Jesus Christ is a lifelong experience. Learning to listen intently for God's message to you in Scripture, story, the events of the day, and your times of silence and prayer will open your mind and heart to the best ways for you to access and receive the mentoring of God.

One tool that can help you learn to listen with intent is note-taking. This week, be even more intentional in the Reflect and Respond segments of the prayer pattern. Spend more time listening for and recording the urgings, cautions, and encouragements of the Holy Spirit, as well as the specific actions you are prompted to take.

If you desire, consider expanding your note-taking to more in-depth journaling. Use the pages provided at the end of the book or a separate notebook or journal. Write out your prayers and what you hear God saying to you. Note specific petitions and answers to prayer. Over time, a prayer journal can help you to see how God is speaking and working in your life.

We learn to listen so that we will not miss the most important voice of all time with the most important message we will ever hear.

Rueben P. Job, *When You Pray*

A Trusted Mentor
Daily Prayer Pattern

Prayer of Presence

> *Lover of all who are lost,*
> *Uncertain and alone,*
> *Confused and frightened,*
> *Arrogant and disrespectful,*
> *Anxious and fearful,*
> *All who are seeking a safe and secure home,*
> *And all who are already*
> > *comfortably at home in your presence,*
>
> *Come to me now and*
> *Make yourself known to me*
> *As I seek to quiet the noise of the world,*
> *The anxiety of my heart and mind,*
> *And the call of unfinished tasks*
> *So that I may recognize and welcome your voice,*
> *Embrace your presence,*
> *Understand your call,*
> *And invite you to change me more and more*
> *Into that wonderful image you have of me*
> *As your faithful, loving,*
> > *and obedient child.*

Silence

Gently lay aside the thoughts that seek to divide your attention and focus on the holy Presence in which you abide. Sit in silence as you quiet your soul before God.

Scripture

Monday	John 10:1-7
Tuesday	Acts 1:21-26
Wednesday	Luke 4:1-4
Thursday	Romans 12:1-2
Friday	Colossians 2:6-9
Saturday	1 John 1:1-4
Sunday	Psalm 139:1-10

Turn to the Daily Scriptures section to read the day's text from the Common English Bible.

Reading

On the first day of your week, read the story found in the Weekly Reading section. Pay attention to the details of the story and the main truth it contains. Look for ways in which the story on the page relates to the story of your life.

On each day following, recall the story and consider any new insights or applications. You also may choose to read and reflect on the quotations interspersed throughout Week 3.

Dialogue and Discovery
What is the Scripture passage saying to me today?
Can I accept and apply this message to myself? To my world?
How will this message change my life?
What is the reading revealing to me today?
What messages does the reading call forth from my own story?
What direction, guidance, or wisdom am I hearing and sensing?
What actions are being suggested as my response?

Reflection
Be even more intentional this week as you listen to and reflect on God's communication to you through silence, prayer, Scripture, and story. Spend more time listening not only for the obvious messages but also for the subtle whispers. Make careful notes of all that you are hearing. If you are so inclined, consider expanding your notes in the journaling pages at the end of the book or in a separate notebook or journal, recording your dialogue with God in greater detail.

Insights and Thoughts:

Response
After you have recorded what you are hearing, give particular attention to what response that message is inviting. Be intentional as you describe the specific actions you will take.

Today I will...

Prayers of Petition
For the world, its leaders, and its people
For those whose lives touch mine today
For myself and those placed in my care
The prayer Jesus taught us

Blessing
God of love beyond my comprehension, hold me close so that I may be as aware of the beat of your heart of love as I am of the beat of my own heart as you guide me through the day.

If you know who you are, you'll know what to do.

Integrity involves wholeness and authenticity. It is living a life consistent with who I am within. It is living a life that requires my thoughts, my feelings and my actions to be congruent, to be the union of who I am within—what I believe, who I understand myself to be and how I live my life.

Ronald J. Greer, *If You Know Who You Are You'll Know What to Do*

*Your word is a lamp before my feet
and a light for my journey.*

Psalm 119:105

Daily Scriptures

Monday *John 10:1-7*

"I assure you that whoever doesn't enter into the sheep pen through the gate but climbs over the wall is a thief and an outlaw. The one who enters through the gate is the shepherd of the sheep. The guard at the gate opens the gate for him, and the sheep listen to his voice. He calls his own sheep by name and leads them out. Whenever he has gathered all of his sheep, he goes before them and they follow him, because they know his voice. They won't follow a stranger but will run away because they don't know the stranger's voice." Those who heard Jesus use this analogy didn't understand what he was saying.

So Jesus spoke again, "I assure you that I am the gate of the sheep."

Discernment comes naturally to those who spend enough time aware of God's presence to learn to trust God and desire God's will above all else.

Rueben P. Job

Tuesday   Acts 1:21-26

"Therefore, we must select one of those who have accompanied us during the whole time the Lord Jesus lived among us, beginning from the baptism of John until the day when Jesus was taken from us. This person must become along with us a witness to his resurrection." So they nominated two: Joseph called Barsabbas, who was also known as Justus, and Matthias.

They prayed, "Lord, you know everyone's deepest thoughts and desires. Show us clearly which one you have chosen from among these two to take the place of this ministry and apostleship, from which Judas turned away to go to his own place." When they cast lots, the lot fell on Matthias. He was added to the eleven apostles.

❧

Wednesday   Luke 4:1-4

Jesus returned from the Jordan River full of the Holy Spirit, and was led by the Spirit into the wilderness. There he was tempted for forty days by the devil. He ate nothing during those days and afterward Jesus was starving. The devil said to him, "Since you are God's Son, command this stone to become a loaf of bread."

Jesus replied, "It's written, *People won't live only by bread.*"

❦

Thursday   *Romans 12:1-2*

So, brothers and sisters, because of God's mercies, I encourage you to present your bodies as a living sacrifice that is holy and pleasing to God. This is your appropriate priestly service. Don't be conformed to the patterns of this world, but be transformed by the renewing of your minds so that you can figure out what God's will is—what is good and pleasing and mature.

Early in the life of the Christian faith persons seeking discernment were mentored in the discipline of *indifference*. That is, they were urged to come to the place of seeking only God's will as the result of their discernment. When we are closely bound to God in Christ this becomes our normal response.

Rueben P. Job

Friday   *Colossians 2:6-9*

So live in Christ Jesus the Lord in the same way as you received him. Be rooted and built up in him, be established in faith, and overflow with thanksgiving just as you were taught. See to it that nobody enslaves you with philosophy and foolish deception, which conform to human traditions and the way the world thinks and acts rather than Christ. All the fullness of deity lives in Christ's body.

❧

Saturday   *1 John 1:1-4*

We announce to you what existed from the beginning, what we have heard, what we have seen with our eyes, what we have seen and our hands handled, about the word of life. The life was revealed, and we have seen, and we testify and announce to you the eternal life that was with the Father and was revealed to us. What we have seen and heard, we also announce it to you so that you can have fellowship with us. Our fellowship is with the Father and with his Son, Jesus Christ. We are writing these things so that our joy can be complete.

We have often seen children take on the qualities of their parents and students begin to reflect in their lives the life and ways of their teachers. To live in an intimate relationship with Christ is to begin to act like Christ, to think like Christ, and to be Christ-like in all of our living.

Rueben P. Job, *A Wesleyan Spiritual Reader*

Sunday *Psalm 139:1-10*

Lord, you have examined me.
> You know me.
You know when I sit down and when I stand up.
> Even from far away, you comprehend my plans.
You study my traveling and resting.
> You are thoroughly familiar with all my ways.
There isn't a word on my tongue, LORD,
> that you don't already know completely.
You surround me—front and back.
> You put your hand on me.
That kind of knowledge is too much for me;
> It's so high above me that I can't fathom it.

Where could I go to get away from your spirit?

Where could I go to escape your presence?
If I went up to heaven, you would be there.
    If I went down to the grave, you would be there too!
If I could fly on the wings of dawn,
       stopping to rest only on the far side of the ocean—
            even there your hand would guide me;
            even there your strong hand would hold
              me tight!

Weekly Reading

I was a typical teenage boy trying to learn how to operate the family farm. My father had experienced a heart attack, and I had just dropped out of high school to do the work my father could no longer do. World War II was raging. My oldest brother was working for the atomic energy plant in Washington State, and the brother next to me was serving in the U. S. Navy, so it seemed right that I would be the one to maintain our family farm.

Because of my loving relationship with my father, I had followed him everywhere all my life and had learned a lot about farming in the northern plains. However, there was much more to learn, and my father became my constant mentor. Even though he was physically very weak, he was always available to gently guide me as I learned how to apply the correct amount of seed to the acre of the various grains we grew. And then at harvest time he showed me how to set the combine for each of those grains and, in doing so, to separate all the grain from the straw.

Often he would sit where we stored the milk as I operated the milking machines, and sometimes he would take a late evening ride with me as I hauled a load of grain to the elevator after the harvesting and chores for the day were completed. In those times he would gracefully guide the conversation to what was coming next on the farming agenda and give me ideas on how to successfully accomplish what I would be facing in the future. He was a wise mentor, and because of our relationship it always seemed like a wonderful partnership.

The good news of the gospel affirms that those of us who follow Jesus have a wise Mentor who is always with us and always ready to teach us everything we need to know.

Some will be quick to tell us that we cannot know the mind of Christ because there is a huge, unbridgeable gap that separates us from God, whom we have come to know through Jesus Christ. Still others tell us we can only hear and respond to God's voice in community, because the Scriptures tell us the church is the body of Christ in the world. There are even some who suggest elaborate exercises and secret knowledge are the only way we can hear and respond to the call of God.

However, Scripture and experience suggest something else. Relationship is the key to hearing, understanding, and responding to the call of God; and that relationship is what God desires, offers, and invites us to enjoy. Jesus reminds us that he knows us, that he calls us by name, and that we will recognize his voice and follow him to life at its fullest (John 10:1-10).

This promise is not for the elite but for everyone. The promise is given to you and to me today, just as we are and not as we will one day become. This marvelous good news is for everyone, and all we need to do is claim it for ourselves.

How will we practice listening, hearing, following, and embracing life at its fullest? We practice by simply developing a way of life that permits time and space to listen, hear, respond, and rejoice in the gift of companionship with God in Christ. Prayer is the foundation of such a way of living.

The God who knows you by name invites you to follow your constant Companion and Guide so that you may claim the most wonderful life possible—a life that is already yours as a child of God. Prayer is the communication connection that makes all of this possible.

We are like children being taught a job by a loving parent who teaches by allowing us to help with the job. And what is such guidance to a child by a parent worth unless there is an eager, but docile, response on the part of the child? The whole value of an interior life depends on this: that no bit of it ever is done alone because we think we know how, but always in response to the gentle guidance and teaching of God.

Evelyn Underhill, *The Ways of the Spirit*

Prayer Practice

Meditation

For centuries meditation has been associated with holy reading, or *lectio divina*. *Lectio divina* is the practice of reading a section of Scripture and then meditating and praying on it. This ancient prayer practice helps us to listen for and understand God's revelation as it restores and renews our trust in and love for God.

Each day this week you are encouraged to select a portion of the daily Scripture passage and meditate on it for at least 5 minutes (10-15 minutes would be ideal, if you have the time).

Read the passage slowly and make notes of anything that seems significant. Think deeply about the text, visualizing any scenes or writing about your understanding of the passage. Pray about what it means for you specifically. Sit silently, listening and communing with God.

Meditating on God's revelation in creation can also be a restorative practice. This week take a walk or sit outside and observe the beauty of God's creation. Both of these ways of meditating on God's revelation can open us to the Holy Spirit's desire to invade our mind and heart and further develop our relationship with God as revealed in Jesus Christ. Take time each day to meditate on God's revelation, allowing your soul to be renewed and refreshed.

Prayer is an invitation to God to intervene in our lives, to let His will prevail in our affairs.

Abraham J. Heschel, *I Asked for Wonder*

EVERYONE NEEDS HELP

Daily Prayer Pattern

Prayer of Presence
Time and space permitting, go outside or sit by a window so that you can behold God's revelation in creation as you pray.

> *God,*
> *Greater than anything I can imagine,*
> *Holiness purer and more brilliant than light,*
> *Mercy that forgives, redeems, and leads to righteousness,*
> *Love that accepts and embraces me just as I am,*
> *Grace that sustains and molds me into more than I am,*
> *Promised presence that will never forsake or leave me alone,*
>
> *I tremble in awe of such greatness and love;*
> *I fall on my knees in gratitude and humility;*
> *I yield my will to yours;*
> *I declare that I am yours alone*
> *and invite you to do with me what you will*
> *As I walk in the light and life*
> *of your unfailing presence.*

Silence

Give thanks for this Holy Presence in which you are always immersed, and be still and listen. Quiet the voices that call for your attention and listen carefully for the voice of the One who loves you more than you can comprehend, who is as near as the air you breathe, and who has promised to be with you always. Wait in silence as you quiet your soul before God.

Scripture

Monday	Romans 8:12-17
Tuesday	Romans 8:22-25
Wednesday	Romans 8:26-28
Thursday	Psalm 25:1-6
Friday	Romans 8:31-34
Saturday	Philippians 2:1-5
Sunday	1 John 4:7-10

Turn to the Daily Scriptures section to read the day's text from the Common English Bible. Select a portion of the Scripture passage and meditate on it for at least 5 minutes using the method described on page 70. (Note: if you have the time, allow 10-15 minutes for the practice of meditation each day this week.)

Reading

On the first day of your week, read the story found in the Weekly Reading section. Pay attention to the details of the story and the main truth it contains. Look for ways in which the story on the page relates to the story of your life.

On each day following, recall the story and consider any new insights or applications. You also may choose to read and reflect on the quotations interspersed throughout Week 4.

Dialogue and Discovery

What is the Scripture passage saying to me today?
Can I accept and apply this message to myself? To my world?
How will this message change my life?
What is the reading revealing to me today?
What messages does the reading call forth from my own story?
What direction, guidance, or wisdom am I hearing and sensing?
What actions are being suggested as my response?
What is the Scripture passage saying to me today?

Reflection

Insights and Thoughts:

Response
Today I will . . .

Prayers of Petition
For the world, its leaders, and its people
For those whose lives touch mine today
For myself and those placed in my care
The prayer Jesus taught us

Blessing
> *Creator of all that exists and lover of all you have made,*
> *Bless me with eyes to see your presence in the world you love,*
> *Ears to hear your tender voice of guidance,*
> *And courage to say, "Here I am, use me this day*
> *for I am yours."*

We will be led from moment to moment into greater light as we see, by increased faith, hope and love, God's loving presence in all events.

Complete abandonment and childlike trust are the Holy Spirit's gifts to those who are ready to die to their false selves and begin to live in the truth of the new creatures that they are and always have been in the eyes of the heavenly Father.

George A. Maloney, *In Jesus We Trust*

"Happy rather are those who hear God's word and put it into practice."

Luke 11:28

Daily Scriptures

So then, brothers and sisters, we have an obligation, but it isn't an obligation to ourselves to live our lives on the basis of selfishness. If you live on the basis of selfishness, you are going to die. But if you put to death the actions of the body with the Spirit, you will live. All who are led by God's Spirit are God's sons and daughters. You didn't receive a spirit of slavery to lead you back again into fear, but you received a Spirit that shows you are adopted as his children. With this Spirit, we cry, "Abba, Father." The same Spirit agrees with our spirit, that we are God's children. But if we are children, we are also heirs. We are God's heirs and fellow heirs with Christ, if we really suffer with him so that we can also be glorified with him.

❦

We know that the whole creation is groaning together and suffering labor pains up until now. And it's not only the creation. We ourselves who have the Spirit as the first crop of the harvest also groan inside as we wait to be adopted and for our bodies to be set free. We were saved in hope. If we see what we hope for, that isn't hope. Who hopes for what they already see? But if we hope for what we don't see, we wait for it with patience.

Do not be surprised or scandalized by the sinful and the tragic. Do what you can to be peace and to do justice, but never expect or demand perfection on this earth. It usually leads to a false moral outrage, a negative identity, intolerance, paranoia, and self-serving crusades against "the contaminating element," instead of "becoming a new creation" ourselves (Gal. 6:15).

Richard Rohr, *Everything Belongs*

❦

Wednesday   Romans 8:26-28

In the same way, the Spirit comes to help our weakness. We don't know what we should pray, but the Spirit himself pleads our case with unexpressed groans. The one who searches hearts knows how the Spirit thinks, because he pleads for the saints, consistent with God's will. We know that God works all things together for good for the ones who love God, for those who are called according to his purpose.

Thursday   *Psalm 25:1-6*

I offer my life to you, Lord.
    My God, I trust you.
Please don't let me be put to shame!
    Don't let my enemies rejoice over me!
For that matter,
    don't let anyone who hopes in you
        be put to shame;
instead, let those who are treacherous without excuse
    be put to shame.

Make your ways known to me, Lord;
    teach me your paths.
Lead me in your truth—teach it to me—
    because you are the God who saves me.
        I put my hope in you all day long.
Lord, remember your compassion and faithful love—
    they are forever!

❦

Friday   *Romans 8:31-34*

So what are we going to say about these things? If God
is for us, who is against us? He didn't spare his own Son but

gave him up for us all. Won't he also freely give us all things with him?

Who will bring a charge against God's elect people? It is God who acquits them. Who is going to convict them? It is Christ Jesus who died, even more, who was raised, and who also is at God's right side. It is Christ Jesus who also pleads our case for us.

❦

Saturday   *Philippians 2:1-5*

Therefore, if there is any encouragement in Christ, any comfort in love, any sharing in the Spirit, any sympathy, complete my joy by thinking the same way, having the same love, being united, and agreeing with each other. Don't do anything for selfish purposes, but with humility think of others as better than yourselves. Instead of each person watching out for their own good, watch out for what is better for others. Adopt the attitude that was in Christ Jesus.

To the degree that we Christians surrender ourselves freely to the leadership of Jesus Christ through the mystical oneness we enjoy with him and in him, to that degree we can say we are Christians, living members of his body. We will know experientially that we live in his light by the gentle love we have toward each person whom we meet in each moment.

George A. Maloney, *In Jesus We Trust*

Sunday   *1 John 4:7-10*

Dear friends, let's love each other, because love is from God, and everyone who loves is born from God and knows God. The person who doesn't love does not know God, because God is love. This is how the love of God is revealed to us: God has sent his only Son into the world so that we can live through him. This is love: it is not that we loved God but that he loved us and sent his Son as the sacrifice that deals with our sins.

I will never forget your precepts
because through them you gave me life again.
I'm yours—save me because I've pursued your precepts!
Psalm 119:93-94

Weekly Reading

It is true that each one of us, no matter how capable, competent, and self-assured we are, needs help now and then. However, as this story by Ronald J. Greer points out, sometimes God sends that help in unexpected ways and from unexpected sources.

❧

I was sitting in the Atlanta airport, waiting at Gate 32 to board a plane. Zones 1 and 2 were called; I stood, picked up my briefcase, and walked toward the line that was forming. As I passed a row of seats I heard a girl ask her mother, "Do I stand up now?"

Something about the girl's voice got my attention. She was developmentally disabled. I kept walking, got in line, and boarded the plane.

I took my place in seat 7C. After I settled in, I looked up. There was the girl, coming down the aisle by herself. I was surprised to see that she was a teenager—she was so petite that she appeared almost frail. The seat in front of mine was hers.

Then "Animal House" boarded. A group of college students came down the aisle and took several rows of seats across from us. They were laughing, joking with one another, and having a great time. But above all else, they were being cool. Cool, you understand, was imperative.

Finally, the plane was pushed back and began taxiing. Ten minutes later the pilot announced that we were cleared for takeoff. He made the final turn onto the runway.

I looked up and saw that little head with the brunette hair lean partway across the aisle. I heard the girl say to the college student across from her, "I get real nervous when we take off. Would you hold my hand?"

My eyes were riveted on the young man to see what he would do. Holding a stranger's hand is not cool. After an initial nervous blush, he began to smile, and halfway across the aisle came that kid's big ol' hand. The girl's tiny hand grabbed it and squeezed.

There they held hands, across the aisle, as our Delta jet was airborne.

There they held hands as I stared, also in disbelief, and memorized that sacred moment. I knew I was witnessing a sacrament.

The plane's wheels clunked into place beneath us. She let go of his hand and said something to him. The engines were now so loud, I couldn't hear.

For the next hour and a half he read his Harry Potter book. She listened to her iPod.

Then the plane descended as we approached Shreveport. In those few moments, as we anticipated the jolt of the runway, this young man turned to the girl and—as I read his lips—asked, "Do you need to hold my hand?"

Apparently she said, "No." He smiled and nodded.

Ronald J. Greer, *If You Know Who You Are*
You'll Know What to Do

Now disciples of Jesus are people who want to take into their being the order of The Kingdom Among Us. They wish to live their lives in it as Jesus himself would, and that requires internalization of that order. Study is the chief way in which they do it. They devote their attention, their thoughtful inquiry, and their practical experimentation to the order of the kingdom as seen in Jesus, in the written word of Scripture, in others who walk in the way, and, indeed, in every good thing in nature, history, and culture.

Dallas Willard, *The Divine Conspiracy*

Prayer Practice

Remembering God's Love

Remembering and reflecting on God's love is a simple but vital prayer practice that enables us to receive and respond to the Holy Spirit's presence and invitation to be our Companion and Guide.

During your prayer time this week, and throughout each day, remind yourself often that you are God's beloved daughter or son. This practice will enable you to claim your inheritance and live as a child of God. To help guide you in this practice, you will find prompts in the Daily Prayer Pattern instructing you to mark or underline words and phrases in the Scriptures and readings that assure you of this truth. During the Response segment of your prayer time, write these words on an index card or on a note in your phone or tablet so that you may refer to them throughout the day to maintain your awareness of God's loving presence.

Today, instead of getting stressed out because I have too much to do, I will ask God to guide me in my yes and no to tasks and opportunities that come my way. And then I will ask God to inspire, bless, and grant wisdom, energy, and strength beyond my own to do what God has placed in my hands to accomplish.

Rueben P. Job, *When You Pray*

WEEK. 5

FLYING SOLO

Daily Prayer Pattern

Prayer of Presence

> *Creator God*
> *Whose name is love,*
> *Who made all that is*
> *And is creating still,*
>
> *Who nurtures and sustains all that is,*
> *Seeks me with clear and tender invitation,*
> *Desiring my constant attentiveness*
> > *so that I may hear every gentle word*
> > *of guidance, assurance, and love*
> *As I am offered my full inheritance*
> > *as a child of the living God,*
>
> *Speak to me now as I listen*
> > *for your word of truth,*
> *For I am yours and desire to*
> *Live as your faithful child this day*
> > *and always.*

Silence

Dismiss your thoughts of tasks to be done and schedules to meet, and open your mind and heart to hear and receive God's loving presence and guidance. Sit in silence as you quiet your soul before God, inviting the Spirit's guidance to form your prayers and shape your life.

Scripture

Monday	Acts 8:26-29
Tuesday	Psalm 32:8-11
Wednesday	John 14:23-26
Thursday	Isaiah 58:6-11
Friday	James 1:2-5
Saturday	John 16:12-16
Sunday	Ephesians 2:8-10

Turn to the Daily Scriptures section to read the day's text from the Common English Bible. As you read the passage, underline words and phrases that remind and assure you of God's love for you and for all the world.

Reading

On the first day of your week, read the story found in the Weekly Reading section. Pay attention to the details of the story and the main truth it contains. Look for ways in which the story on the page relates to the story of your life. As you read, underline words and phrases that remind and assure you of God's love for you and for all the world.

On each day following, recall the story and consider any new insights or applications. You also may choose to read and reflect on the quotations interspersed throughout Week 5.

Dialogue and Discovery

What is the Scripture passage saying to me today?
Can I accept and apply this message to myself? To my world?
How will this message change my life?
What is the reading revealing to me today?
What messages does the reading call forth from my own story?
What direction, guidance, or wisdom am I hearing and sensing?
What actions are being suggested as my response?

Reflection
Insights and Thoughts:

Response
Today I will . . .

Take a moment now to write the words and phrases you underlined in the Scripture and reading(s) on an index card or in a note in your phone or tablet. Remember to refer to them throughout the day to maintain your awareness of God's loving presence with you.

Prayers of Petition
For the world, its leaders, and its people
For those whose lives touch mine today
For myself and those placed in my care
The prayer Jesus taught us

Blessing
Faithful Guide and Companion, continue to speak to me the words of guidance, correction, encouragement, and love that I need. And send me to meet this day with your power and presence to go where Jesus Christ leads me and live as your faithful disciple all day long.

God created us for union with Himself: This is the original purpose of our lives. And God is defined as love (1 John 4:16). Living in awareness of our belovedness is the axis around which the Christian life revolves. Being the beloved is our identity, the core of our existence. It is not merely a lofty thought, an inspiring idea, or one name among many. It is the name by which God knows us and the way He relates to us.

Brennan Manning, *Abba's Child*

Turn your ear and hear the words of the wise;
focus your mind on my knowledge.

Proverbs 22:17

Daily Scriptures

Monday   *Acts 8:26-29*

An angel from the Lord spoke to Philip, "At noon, take the road that leads from Jerusalem to Gaza." (This is a desert road.) So he did. Meanwhile, an Ethiopian man was on his way home from Jerusalem, where he had come to worship. He was a eunuch and an official responsible for the entire treasury of Candace. (Candace is the title given to the Ethiopian queen.) He was reading the prophet Isaiah while sitting in his carriage. The Spirit told Philip, "Approach this carriage and stay with it."

❧

Tuesday   *Psalm 32:8-11*

I will instruct you and teach you
    about the direction you should go.
    I'll advise you and keep my eye on you.
Don't be like some senseless
    horse or mule,
    whose movement must be controlled
    with a bit and a bridle.
    Don't be anything like that!

The pain of the wicked is severe,
    but faithful love surrounds
    the one who trusts the LORD.
You who are righteous,
    rejoice in the LORD and be glad!
    All you whose hearts are right,
    sing out in joy!

The power by which God transforms humans is the Holy Spirit. Christian spirituality is therefore not a matter of cultivating some dimension of the human spirit, but a matter of obedient response to the Spirit of God.

Luke Timothy Johnson, *The Creed*

Wednesday   *John 14:23-26*

Jesus answered, "Whoever loves me will keep my word. My Father will love them, and we will come to them and make our home with them. Whoever doesn't love me doesn't keep my words. The word that you hear isn't mine. It is the word of the Father who sent me.

"I have spoken these things to you while I am with you. The Companion, the Holy Spirit, whom the Father will send in my name, will teach you everything and will remind you of everything I told you."

❦

Thursday   *Isaiah 58:6-11*

Isn't this the fast I choose:
    releasing wicked restraints,
        untying the ropes of a yoke,
    setting free the mistreated,
    and breaking every yoke?
Isn't it sharing your bread
    with the hungry
    and bringing the homeless poor
        into your house,
covering the naked when you see them,
and not hiding from your own family?
Then your light
    will break out like the dawn,
    and you will be healed quickly.
Your own righteousness
    will walk before you,
    and the LORD's glory
        will be your rear guard.
Then you will call,
    and the LORD will answer;
    you will cry for help,
        and God will say, "I'm here."

If you remove the yoke from among you,
    the finger-pointing, the wicked speech;
if you open your heart to the hungry,
    and provide abundantly
        for those who are afflicted,
    your light will shine in the darkness,
    and your gloom will be like the noon.
The LORD will guide you continually
    and provide for you,
        even in parched places.
    He will rescue your bones.
You will be like a watered garden,
    like a spring of water
        that won't run dry.

Friday   *James 1:2-5*

My brothers and sisters, think of the various tests you encounter as occasions for joy. After all, you know that the testing of your faith produces endurance. Let this endurance complete its work so that you may be fully mature, complete, and lacking in nothing. But anyone who needs wisdom should ask God, whose very nature is to give to everyone without a second thought, without keeping score. Wisdom will certainly be given to those who ask.

Be bold enough to ask God to transform your own life and invest your life as leaven to transform the world where you are. Begin every day in seeking God's direction and companionship, and end every day in offering anew all you have done and all that you are to the One who gives you life.

Rueben P. Job, *A Wesleyan Spiritual Reader*

Saturday   *John 16:12-16*

"I have much more to say to you, but you can't handle it now. However, when the Spirit of Truth comes, he will guide you in all truth. He won't speak on his own, but will say whatever he hears and will proclaim to you what is to come. He will glorify me, because he will take what is mine and proclaim it to you. Everything that the Father has is mine. That's why I said that the Spirit takes what is mine and will proclaim it to you. Soon you won't be able to see me; soon after that, you will see me."

Sunday   *Ephesians 2:8-10*

You are saved by God's grace because of your faith. This salvation is God's gift. It's not something you possessed. It's not something you did that you can be proud of. Instead, we are God's accomplishment, created in Christ Jesus to do good things. God planned for these good things to be the way that we live our lives.

Weekly Reading

He patted me on the shoulder and said, "Make three touch-and-go landings and takeoffs, and if all goes well, I will wave you off, and you will be free to go out ten miles and fly solo until your hour scheduled for the plane is up." My instructor pilot calmly got out of the plane, securely closed the door, and walked off the runway; and I took off on my first ever solo flight.

I was surprised at how easily the plane became airborne without the 175 pounds of my instructor in the back seat. I made the three touch-and-go landings and takeoffs, received a salute and a wave from my instructor, and was off for an exhilarating look at the city and the surrounding countryside from an altitude of 2,000 feet.

I was cautious not to get too close to the "no fly zone" around the Air Force base to my north, and I followed the routine of sweeping my eyes across the air space that surrounded me and the instruments in front of me as I had been instructed. I was also careful to pick out an emergency landing spot in the event that something unexpected happened and I was forced to land before returning to the airport.

The time went swiftly, and soon I entered the landing pattern, made a good landing, and taxied in to refuel the plane before signing out. The paperwork for my student pilot's license was soon complete, and plans were made for my first long-distance solo flight.

Reflecting on my experience, I wondered how my instructor knew when it was time to give me that confident pat on the shoulder and say, "Go out and practice what you have learned in flight school and flight training." I assumed it was because I was a very eager and attentive student, having longed to fly for thirty-five years. But perhaps it was also his desire to build confidence and trust not only in myself but also in the truth I had been taught.

When our relationship with God in Christ is dominated by our longing to be a faithful disciple and we eagerly seek the presence, guidance, and direction that God awaits to give, we will come to that place where we get a "pat on the shoulder," assuring us that our faithful Guide and Savior has prepared us to listen to and trust the teaching that we have treasured in our hearts and minds and the gentle, confident voice that comes to guide and direct our every decision and act.

The very best part is remembering the promises that Jesus makes to each and every one of us:

> *"The Companion, the Holy Spirit, whom the Father will send in my name, will teach you everything and will remind you of everything I told you."*   John 14:26

> *"Whoever loves me will keep my word. My Father will love them, and we will come to them and make our home with them."*   John 14:23

You see, though we move forward in our lives as followers of Christ, growing in our discipleship and putting into practice all we have learned, we never really fly solo. God is always by our side, directing, guiding, and leading us onward.

A new beginning! We must learn to live each day, each hour, yes, each minute as a new beginning, as a unique opportunity to make everything new. Imagine that we could live each moment as a moment pregnant with new life. Imagine that we could live each day as a day full of promises. Imagine that we could walk through the new year always listening to a voice saying to us: "I have a gift for you and can't wait for you to see it!" Imagine . . . we must open our minds and hearts to the voice that resounds through the valleys and hills of our life saying: "Let me show you where I live among my people. My name is 'God-with-you.' I will wipe away all the tears from your eyes; there will be no more death, and no more mourning or sadness. The world of the past has gone" (see Revelation 21:2-5). We must choose to listen to that voice, and every choice will open us a little more to discover new life hidden in the moment, waiting eagerly to be born.

Henri Nouwen, *Here and Now*

Prayer Practice

Attentiveness and Expectancy

A friend once told me about a period in his life when he was being awakened every morning at three A.M. Being a person of prayer, he began asking God for insight into this upsetting experience.

The answer to his prayer came quickly and clearly. "This seems to be the only time I can get your attention." He accepted the answer and began a practice of prayer at three A.M. every morning. He discovered that his life of prayer grew intensely.

Paying attention to everything that is happening in your life and viewing circumstances, situations, and experiences through "spiritual eyes" can be a helpful prayer practice. Be alert for those moments when you sense God is seeking your attention each day. Give attention to what you discovered; then respond, expecting God to work in your life.

This week, practice attentiveness and expectancy, anticipating unexpected insights or realizations. Pay attention to connections between things you are reading, hearing, or seeing. You will find an additional question in the Dialogue and Discovery segment of the Daily Prayer Pattern to guide you in this process. By approaching prayer with attentiveness and expectancy, you will position yourself to receive from God.

How do we position ourselves today to receive God's love, presence, power, and grace? Faithful Christians of every nation, culture, and age have found that one can become present to God and receive the gifts of God who is always present to us.

Rueben P. Job

GETTING INTO POSITION

Daily Prayer Pattern

Prayer of Presence

> *God revealed in so many ways—*
> *The beauty and magnificence of creation,*
> *The words of prophet, priest, and servant,*
> *The life, death, resurrection of Jesus,*
> *The power and constant presence of your Spirit,*
> *The witness of your servant saints, and*
> *Your sustaining grace that gives me life —*
>
> *I bring myself into your presence*
> *Not to tell you what to do*
> *But to invite you to be my honored guest*
> *As I offer to you all that I am,*
> *All that I hope to become,*
> *And invite your transforming presence*
> *To shape me more and more into your*
> *Beloved and faithful child,*
> *For I am yours and I belong to you,*
> *My faithful Savior and Guide.*

Silence

Step back from the inner and outer noise of the day. Dismiss every interruption of sound or thought about what's next on your calendar and bring your whole being into the presence of God, who is already present to you. Sit in silence as you quiet your soul before God, inviting the Spirit's guidance to form your prayers and shape your life.

Scripture

Monday	Luke 3:21-22
Tuesday	Mark 14:32-37
Wednesday	Luke 11:1-4
Thursday	Luke 19:45-47
Friday	Acts 2:1-4
Saturday	Acts 2:43-47
Sunday	Luke 22:14-20

Turn to the Daily Scriptures section to read the day's text from the Common English Bible.

Reading

On the first day of your week, read the story found in the Weekly Reading section. Pay attention to the details of the story and the main truth it contains. Look for ways in which the story on the page relates to the story of your life.

On each day following, recall the story and consider any new insights or applications. You also may choose to read and reflect on the quotations interspersed throughout Week 6.

Dialogue and Discovery
What is the Scripture passage saying to me today?
Can I accept and apply this message to myself? To my world?
How will this message change my life?
What is the reading revealing to me today?
What messages does the reading call forth from my own story?
What connections can I see between the circumstances, situations, and happenings of my life and the messages I have received from today's readings?
What direction, guidance, or wisdom am I hearing and sensing?
What actions are being suggested as my response?

Reflection
Insights and Thoughts:

Response
Today I will ...

Prayers of Petition
For the world, its leaders, and its people
For those whose lives touch mine today
For myself and those placed in my care
The prayer Jesus taught us

Blessing
>*God of promise, power, and presence,*
>*Be my ever-present Companion and Guide*
>*So that this day and always*
>*I may be your faithful servant child.*

When Jesus is with us, all is right with the world and nothing seems difficult; when he is missing, everything is hard. When Jesus does not speak to the heart, comfort is worthless; but if he speaks only one word, we feel great joy.

William C. Creasy, *The Imitation of Christ, A Timeless Classic for Contemporary Readers*

The word is near you, in your mouth and in your heart.

Romans 10:8

Daily Scriptures

Monday   *Luke 3:21-22*

When everyone was being baptized, Jesus also was baptized. While he was praying, heaven was opened and the Holy Spirit came down on him in bodily form like a dove. And there was a voice from heaven: "You are my Son, whom I dearly love; in you I find happiness."

❦

Tuesday   *Mark 14:32-37*

Jesus and his disciples came to a place called Gethsemane. Jesus said to them, "Sit here while I pray." He took Peter, James, and John along with him. He began to feel despair and was anxious. He said to them, "I'm very sad. It's as if I'm dying. Stay here and keep alert." Then he went a short distance farther and fell to the ground. He prayed that, if possible, he might be spared the time of suffering. He said, "Abba, Father, for you all things are possible. Take this cup of suffering away from me. However—not what I want but what you want."

He came and found them sleeping. He said to Peter, "Simon, are you asleep? Couldn't you stay alert for one hour?"

There is no more plaintive or heartfelt prayer than the cry of Jesus: "My God, My God, why hast thou forsaken me?" (Matt. 27:46b, KJV). Jesus' experience on the cross was, of course, utterly unique and unrepeatable, for he was taking into himself the sin of the world. But in our own way you and I will pray this Prayer of the Forsaken if we seek the intimacy of perpetual communion with the Father. Times of seeming desertion and absence and abandonment appear to be universal among those who have walked this path of faith before us.

Richard Foster, *Prayer: Finding the Heart's True Home*

❦

Wednesday   *Luke 11:1-4*

Jesus was praying in a certain place. When he finished, one of his disciples said, "Lord, teach us to pray, just as John taught his disciples."

Jesus told them, "When you pray, say:

    'Father, uphold the holiness of your name.

    Bring in your kingdom.

    Give us the bread we need for today.

    Forgive us our sins,

        for we also forgive everyone who has wronged us.

    And don't lead us into temptation.' "

❧

Thursday   *Luke 19:45-47*

When Jesus entered the temple, he threw out those who were selling things there. He said to them, "It's written, *My house will be a house of prayer, but you have made it a hideout for crooks.*"

Jesus was teaching daily in the temple. The chief priests, the legal experts, and the foremost leaders among the people were seeking to kill him.

❧

Friday   *Acts 2:1-4*

When Pentecost Day arrived, they were all together in one place. Suddenly a sound from heaven like the howling of a fierce wind filled the entire house where they were sitting. They saw what seemed to be individual flames of fire alighting on each one of them. They were all filled with the Holy Spirit and began to speak in other languages as the Spirit enabled them to speak.

Saturday   *Acts 2:43-47*

A sense of awe came over everyone. God performed many wonders and signs through the apostles. All the believers were united and shared everything. They would sell pieces of property and possessions and distribute the proceeds to everyone who needed them. Every day, they met together in the temple and ate in their homes. They shared food with gladness and simplicity. They praised God and demonstrated God's goodness to everyone. The Lord added daily to the community those who were being saved.

As we listen in on Jesus as he talks and then participate with Jesus as he prays, I hope that together we, writer and readers, will develop a discerning aversion to all forms of depersonalizing godtalk and acquire a taste for and skills in the always personal language God uses, even in our conversations and small talk, maybe especially in our small talk, to make and save and bless us one and all.

Eugene Peterson, *Tell It Slant*

Sunday   *Luke 22:14-20*

When the time came, Jesus took his place at the table, and the apostles joined him. He said to them, "I have earnestly desired to eat this Passover with you before I suffer. I tell you, I won't eat it until it is fulfilled in God's kingdom." After taking a cup and giving thanks, he said, "Take this and share it among yourselves. I tell you that from now on I won't drink from the fruit of the vine until God's kingdom has come." After taking the bread and giving thanks, he broke it and gave it to them, saying, "This is my body, which is given for you. Do this in remembrance of me." In the same way, he took the cup after the meal and said, "This cup is the new covenant by my blood, which is poured out for you."

God! My God! It's you—
   I search for you!
   My whole being thirsts for you!
   My body desires you
      in a dry and tired land,
      no water anywhere.

Psalm 63:1

Weekly Reading

I grew up during the Great Depression and Dust Bowl years that forever changed our nation. The Great Depression brought a wealthy nation to never-before-seen poverty. Many of the wealthy and poor lost all their savings, their jobs, and often their businesses, farms, and communities.

The Dust Bowl years with their unending and blinding dust storms swept away population, farms, and businesses as they ground the survivors into ever-deeper poverty. Farmsteads stood deserted everywhere, and unoccupied houses dotted the streets of nearly every village and city.

Our farm survived because we had a deep and productive well that provided an abundance of clean, life-giving water for garden, animals, trees, and family. That well was pumped by a windmill that had an eight-foot wheel mounted on a tall tower to catch the abundant wind typical for that part of our country.

On those occasions when the wind was just a gentle breeze, my father would climb to the top of that tower and squeeze through an opening in the platform that circled the tower. From that position he took hold of the entire mechanism and turned it until the fans of that giant wheel were facing directly into the breeze. Sometimes he would turn the wheel to get it started, and then it would catch the gentle breeze and produce the life-giving water we needed. Without careful positioning, nothing would have happened. Our farmstead would have looked just fine, but it would have dried up and failed without the needed water.

Positioning is also critical to growth in our relationship with Jesus Christ. The gentle breath of the Holy Spirit is always touching us, but it is our responsibility to position ourselves in ways that make it possible to receive the gifts that God waits to bestow upon us.

The risen Christ appeared to the early disciples on many occasions, and Luke recorded one of the instructions Jesus gave to the disciples about positioning: "Look, I'm sending to you what my Father promised, but you are to stay in the city until you have been furnished with heavenly power" (Luke 24:49).

How do we position ourselves today to receive God's love, presence, power, and grace? Faithful Christians of every nation, culture, and age have found that one can become present to God and receive the gifts of God, who is always present to us. The simple pattern of prayer and reflection provided in this book is one way that we may position ourselves to hear God's loving message and, through the gift of the Holy Spirit, be drawn to God in human form that we see in Jesus.

Jesus walks into our daily lives in many ways—sometimes invited and sometimes not; sometimes welcome and sometimes not so welcome. But he always comes, the bearer of good news. Yet how often do our pre-conceived notions, our way of listening, prevent us from hearing him?

M. Basil Pennington, *Seeking His Mind*

Bibliography

Bondi, Roberta C. *In Ordinary Time.* Nashville: Abingdon, 1996, pp. 22-23, 25.

Creasy, William C. *The Imitation of Christ: A Timeless Classic for Contemporary Readers.* Notre Dame, Indiana: Ave Maria Press, 1989, p. 72.

Foster, Richard. *Prayer: Finding the Heart's True Home.* San Francisco: HarperCollins, 1992 (Week 2: p. 1; Week 6: p. 17).

Greer, Ronald J. *If You Know Who You Are You'll Know What to Do.* Nashville: Abingdon, 2009 (Week 3: p. 17; Week 4: pp. 25 26).

Havel, Vaclav. *International Herald Tribune.* Paris, February 21, 1990.

Heschel, Abraham J. *Between God and Man.* New York: Free Press, 1997, p. 211.

_____. *I Asked for Wonder: A Spiritual Anthology.* Samuel H. Dresner, ed. New York: Crossroad, 2001, p. 28.

_____. *Man Is Not Alone.* New York: Farrar, Straus and Giroux, 1976, p. 92.

Job, Rueben P. *A Guide to Spiritual Discernment.* Nashville: Upper Room, 1996, p. 24.

_____. *A Wesleyan Spiritual Reader.* Nashville: Abingdon, 1998 (Week 3: p. 37; Week 5: p. 194).

_____. *When You Pray.* Nashville: Abingdon, 2009 (Week 3: p. 66; Week 5: p. 122).

Johnson, Ben Campbell. *GodSpeech.* Grand Rapids, Michigan: Eerdmans, 2006, p. 30.

Johnson, Luke Timothy. *The Creed: What Christians Believe and Why It Matters.* New York: Image, 2004, p. 245.

Maloney, George A. *In Jesus We Trust.* Notre Dame, Indiana: Ave Maria Press, 1990 (Week 2: pp. 36-37; Week 4: pp. 148-49).

Manning, Brennan. *Abba's Child: The Cry of the Heart for Intimate Belonging.* Colorado Springs: NavPress, 2002, p. 52.

Nouwen, Henri. *Here and Now: Living in the Spirit.* New York: Crossroad, 2006, pp. 16-17.

_____. *In the Name of Jesus.* New York: Crossroad, 1989, p. 69.

Pennington, M. Basil. *Seeking His Mind.* Brewster, Massachusetts: Paraclete, 2002, p. 33.

Peterson, Eugene H. *Tell It Slant: A Conversation on the Language of Jesus in His Stories and Prayers.* Grand Rapids: Eerdmans, 2008, p. 5.

Rohr, Richard. *Everything Belongs.* New York: Crossroad, 2003 (Week 2: p. 29; Week 4: p. 31).

Underhill, Evelyn. *The Ways of the Spirit.* New York: Crossroad, 1993, p. 189.

Wesley, John. "Letter to Mr. John Trembath." *The Works of John Wesley,* Vol. 12. Nashville: Abingdon, 2012, p. 254.

Willard, Dallas. *The Divine Conspiracy: Rediscovering Our Hidden Life in God.* New York: HarperCollins, 1998, p. 361.

Journaling Pages